LifeNet 4 Hope®

For Such a Time as This

The Interwoven History of Crossroads, 100 Huntley St., Circle Square TV & Ranches - and LifeNet 4 Hope

Diane Roblin-Rutledge

Foreword by

Norma-Jean Mainse

For Such a Time as This Soft cover 978-1-896213-30-9
E-book 978-1-896213-29-3
First Date of Publishing - Oct. 1, 2023
Update - Oct. 30, 2024
Publisher - ByDesign Media *www.bydesignmedia.ca*

Author - Diane Roblin-(Lee) Rutledge
Research and development - Diane Roblin-(Lee) Rutledge
Cover and Inter design - Diane Roblin-(Lee) Rutledge

Dedication

The purpose of this little book is to demonstrate the intricacy of God's handiwork as He interwove the lives, circumstances and hearts of people and organizations to reach out to today's confused, lonely and anxious teens and families. It has taken years to weave LifeNet as a tool to reach out with hope and gather precious young people to His heart.

God has been in no rush because He was preparing LifeNet to be used in the most challenging days this world has ever known. Never before have families and young people been faced with such chaos and confusion but LifeNet is now ready to respond - *For Such a Time as This.*

We dedicate this history of LifeNet to today's teens and families in hopes that recognition of God's unwavering love, faithfulness and purpose for their lives will be clearer than ever before.

Diane Roblin-Rutledge
CEO LifeNet Ministries Inc.

Foreword

TO GOD BE THE GLORY – GREAT THINGS HE HAS DONE!

I'm overjoyed to be asked to write a foreword for this miracle story of LifeNet, which has its ministry roots deeply intertwined with those of David and mine.

In this inspiring book, Diane Roblin-Rutledge weaves together the unique historical fabrics of the Mainse, Rutledge and Roblin families, which represent many years of effective ministry across Canada and around the world. You will read of pivotal moments in the ministry that sparked new outreaches, like the one when the heart of my brother Glen Rutledge was broken by the story of a young 12-year-old boy who ended his life by suicide. God used that tragedy to launch us into a TV ministry for children.

I remember well how, for much of the 1980's, Diane's ministry heart shone brightly in the middle of the night as a regular host of our Crossroads program called Nite-Lite, which aired from 2:00-4:30 am each weeknight. And more recently, I was overjoyed when Diane joined our extended family and married my brother Glen in 2021!

I am very proud of Glen and Diane for their vision and tireless work with the LifeNet ministry, as they help precious young people who are confused, hurting, and in a battle for their very lives.

Before David passed away in 2017, he challenged Glen to passionately pursue God's call on his life for reaching out to countless hurting, suicidal young lives who need to know that Jesus loves them and that someone cares.

I am so glad that the Lord has inspired Diane Roblin-Rutledge to put into book form this amazing miracle story of God's faithfulness down through the years.

You will be inspired to trust God to also fulfill the vision He has given you. You just have to take the limits off of God in your thinking and have faith enough to believe!

Norma-Jean Mainse

For Such a Time as This

LifeNet Youth Suicide Prevention

LifeNet / Crossroads /100 Huntley St. / Circle Square

Interwoven History

The Rutledges

The Roblins

Believe it or not, the history of LifeNet Ministries, the youth suicide prevention initiative, stretches all the way back to the early days of the mission-minded Mainse family, the musical Rutledge family and the called-by-His-grace Roblin family. It's a complex but simple story of answers to the prayers of parents and the powerful working of God through their children.

The Mainse Family

David Mainse, who married into the talented Rutledge family, said, "My most vivid memory of my mother is seeing her on her knees, praying for others, and particularly for her husband and children.[1] The offspring of Lillian Davies Rutledge and Grace Irwin Roblin share the same memory of their mothers. The impact of those prayers cannot be overstated. It was the basis for everything hat followed.

In his book, *100 Huntley Street*, David remembered his family having devotions every night after dinner. While family devotions have gone the way of the dinosaur in many families today, they were part of the fabric of the Mainse, Rutledge and Roblin family lives. They were remembered along with Saturday night bath time, the delight of ice cream in a cone at the corner store, gathering eggs from under warm feathers in the mornings and learning to plow a straight furrow. Spending time with the Heavenly Father was part of normal life. It wasn't contrived, scheduled or imposed – it was just part of life. A portion of scripture would be read and then everyone, adults and children, would kneel down by the old sofa and pray. No one ever accused young David of being a goody-two-shoes. He enjoyed mischief and the exuberance of life like any normal, healthy boy (perhaps more than some!), but his character and spirit were infused with the love and personal relationship with his Heavenly Father – and that made all the difference. As the years passed, the importance of prayer remained in David's heart. He listened when God impressed upon him the need to spend equal time in prayer prior to time that would be spent in ministry.

1. Mainse, David, *This Far by Faith*, CCCI, 2013, Burlington ON, p.22

David Mainse became an icon in the world of televangelism. He was honored, with Dr. Billy Graham, for his steadfast integrity throughout his 60 years of ministry and the massive impact he had on the world. He was a brilliant, but humble, heart-to-heart communicator with a pure passion for souls and a powerful sensitivity to the quiet voice of God leading him. His primary purpose in life revolved around his personal witness and ability to reach the world as an expression of God's arms of love. When occasionally confronted by the silence of God in response to his request for guidance, David learned to realize that the assurance of God's love was all he needed. He was simply to go ahead, share his decisions with the Board of Directors for their approval, and God's love would keep him on track to do His will. He commented, "A person does not have to be a spiritual giant to know God's voice, just a sheep who listens and spends time in the presence of the Shepherd."[2]

Lillian Davies Rutledge

In their little tar paper house near Harrisburg, Ontario, Lillian and Godfrey Rutledge prayed for a large musical family that would bring great glory to God. With more instruments than furniture, music became the air the children (Harold, Reynold, Eleanor, Glen, Ralph and Norma-

2. Mainse, David, *This Far by Faith*, CCCI, 2013, Burlington ON, p.60

Jean) breathed. Lillian trusted God for every step of life. Like the Mainse family, the Rutledges included family devotions in their day. After dinner, scripture would be read and then everyone would get down on their knees beside their chairs and pray together. More often than not, someone would sing a line of a chorus or hymn and the others would join in harmony. With no indoor bathroom or running water in their little home, they would pray for a larger home to meet their needs and "conveniences." While the little children didn't really understand the meaning of the word, they knew it was something their parents wanted and so they prayed for "conveniences." One day there was a prayer meeting in Galt (now Cambridge) and the Lord gave a message through the Gifts of the Spirit. The message was that the Lord had heard the prayers of the Rutledge family and they would be given a larger home with conveniences, filled with everything they needed – at no cost to them.

Lillian began to tell the children they would be moving. When the children told the neighbors and questions about their plans were asked, Lillian's response was simply that, yes, they were moving but she didn't know where or when.

Not long after, one of the neighbour men ran through a blizzard to the nearby country school, yelling, "Come, come! We need the big boys to come. The Rutledge house is on fire." Harold, Reynold and 12-year-old Glen grabbed their coats and ran down the snowy road towards their home. In the distance they could see plumes of black smoke and their mother standing at the side of the road with her arm around young Eleanor, watching their humble home, with all their instruments and belongings, burn to the ground like a match box. The first words they heard her say were, "This is all part of God's plan."

With nothing left but the clothes on their backs, the family was given refuge in the homes of several neighbours. The local newspaper headline read, "The Musical Rutledge Family Loses Everything."

A day or two later, at the neighbour's house, Glen overheard his mom lamenting in prayer, in a side room, about the loss of her engagement ring. She said, "Lord You know all about this." She had been doing some canning and put her ring in her purse while she worked. In his tender, young heart, Glen believed that if they were in the middle of God's plan, it wouldn't be too hard for God to return the ring to his mother.

He called young Ralph and Norma-Jean and said, "Come on! We're going to go and get Mother's ring. If we can find her purse, we'll find the ring." The ashes were still smoldering when they arrived at the hole that had once been their home. He told the younger two to start in opposite corners and they'd work towards the centre, kicking up ashes. Before long, Glen's foot kicked up the purse! While the metal clasp was totally warped from the heat, the leather purse was miraculously, somewhat intact. Running to the neighbour's house, they called, "Mother, Mother! We found your purse."

Glen put the purse on the kitchen table and managed to open the warped clasp. Retrieving a little interior change purse, he took out a 10-dollar bill and the ring. The bill had a burn hole where the head of the king should have been. Mother held it up and said, "No earthly man will provide our needs. The King of Kings will supply the miracle." Because the serial number was intact, the bank replaced the 10 dollars.

Then the donations began to flood in from the community. When they were just 200 dollars shy of the price of a home in Cambridge, Godfrey said he'd go to the bank and get a loan, but Lillian said no, that God had promised there would be no cost to them and they needed to wait on His promise. Sure enough, the full amount came in. The house was purchased – with conveniences! When Ralph first went in, he ran upstairs and flushed the toilet. Conveniences! Enough furniture arrived to fill every room. When every room was fully furnished, the donations stopped. Then Lillian decided they needed to have a celebration to share the goodness of God. Cars lined the street as far as one could see, as people arrived to give thanks and glory to God for His faithfulness.

83 Forrest Rd., Cambridge

Stories of miracles like God's instant healing of Godfrey's bleeding ulcers and of his back have echoed across Rutledge family tables down through the years. Following the fire, Godfrey started the "Rutledge Music" store in the living room of their house, once again filling the house with instruments. Admitting that he did not have the faith to commit to renting a store space, Lillian said, "Then do it on my faith." Harold, the eldest, helped build the business while the music of the Rutledge siblings became legendary in the field of gospel music.

The Rutledge Family circa 1950
BR - Reynold, Godfrey, Lillian, Harold, Glen
FR - Eleanor, Ralph, Norma-Jean

To this day, the siblings (all in their 80's and 90's) and their spouses all connect (now on face time Messenger) several times weekly, sharing the family happenings, developments and prayer needs, giving credence to the meme, "The family that prays together, stays together." It's not unusual for one to sing the first line of a song and be joined by the others.

While it might seem that Diane Roblin-Lee, who also married into the Rutledge family, arrived late at the party, not having married Glen until later in life, God's timing was exquisite. As His plan unfolded, it became clear that all the events of her earlier life had been training and preparation to fulfill God's unique purpose and calling on her life.

Diane Roblin-Rutledge

At the age of 33, having been away from the Lord for 15 years, Diane discovered the bleak emptiness of life without Christ. Little did she know, at the time, that her mother, Grace Roblin and her aunt, Jessie Hogan, had committed in January 1978 to fast and pray for her every Monday. As Diane stumbled through efforts to find more purpose to life than she was experiencing, the brand-new program, *100 Huntley Street,* with it's fascinating stories of the joy in knowing Jesus, was there for her. It was out of the amazing transformation she experienced in April that year,[3] that God positioned her in her calling to write[4] and set her on a remarkable Crossroads journey that culminated in her marriage to Glen and the fulfillment of the vision God had given him for reaching out to this generation of teens through LifeNet.

While God never promised life without challenges on this earth, the evidence of His response to the fervent, faithful prayers of loving parents is thrilling. If there's one message to glean from this book, it's the importance of starting prayer early in a family and maintaining it as a core priority. If it's not started early, it can be started later. Mercifully, every generation is given equal opportunity to experience this amazing grace.

---

3. The full story of Diane's return to the Lord is available in *My Father's Child* on Amazon.

4. amzn.to/3C70z6U

The Interwoven History of LifeNet

Youth Suicide Prevention

In order to understand the full picture of the roots of LifeNet, it's necessary to understand several seemingly divergent threads that began to be interwoven in the last half of the last century and were gradually brought together to form a LifeNet that would rescue vulnerable young people and serve as a preemptive measure against tragedy.

The story begins and ends with weddings and will culminate one day soon with the greatest wedding of all time when our Eternal Bridegroom returns to gather all those who truly love Him to celebrate the climax of all of history.

Introduced by Ralph Rutledge in Bible College, David Mainse and Norma-Jean married in1958. Their wedding and the beginning of their ministry was the match that set fire to a tremendous move of God across Canada. Beginning in Brighton, Ontario, it was eventually fueled by the Spirit-filled broadcast evangelism of Crossroads Christian Communications.

The King's Men:
Bob Ostrosser
Glen Rutledge,
Mel Stevens,
Reynold Rutledge &
Don Newman

The desires of Lillian and Godfrey Rutledge's hearts for a large musical family through which God would be glorified were beginning to be fulfilled in exciting ways. As part of The King's Men (a sought-after gospel vocal and instrumental group), Glen and Reynold were performing at meetings throughout the US and Canada.

In the 1950's, The King's Men met Doug Gibb, an Australian businessman deeply concerned about youth issues. He was in Australia when crowds of youth, in response to Billy Graham's meetings, were meeting at dawn on Bondi beach, crying out to God to raise up areas of ministry for their lives.

Brothers Harold and Reynold Rutledge (Harold was part of the King's Men until he left to carry on the Rutledge Music store)

While working overseas in Maryland, Mr. Gibb witnessed a form of dude ranch camping ministry which did not exist in Australia. A vision for its implementation 'down under' began to take shape as an answer to the prayers of the young people for ministry opportunities. This was the beginning of the weaving of multiple God-given visions to reach out to young people. It began the eventual Rutledge involvement in ranch ministry and its consequent impact on Canada and the world.

Through his connection to Don Newman, Doug Gibb challenged the King's Men to join him in Australia to do singing tours to raise money to start the ranch.

The King's Men, having agreed to move to Australia if all their wives were in total agreement, committed to go and stay until the ranch was firmly established.

Ship ahoy!

So it was that Mr. Gibb returned to Australia with the King's Men and their young families.

Driving the travelers to Union Station to catch the train to Vancouver for the ship, Ralph Rutledge sang the chorus, "So Glad I'm Yours Lord." As he sang, God spoke to Glen and told him that it would be the opening song for a daily radio program He would give them in Australia.

Evelyn & Ralph Rutledge

Once on board for the 18-day voyage from Vancouver to Sydney Harbour, the group (in faith) worked on the format of the promised (by God) radio program so that when the Lord would open the doors, they would be ready.

The King's Men

Not long after they arrived, Don Newman organized a youth conference (featuring The King's Men) in the Blue Hills of Australia. During the conference, the group put on a mock radio program where they demonstrated the

potential outreach to raise support and awareness of the ranch ministry to parents and young people. Unbeknown to them, as they were performing the mock program, a father, who had come to pick up his daughter from the conference, was in the audience. He watched the entire presentation and then approached the group at the end. He introduced himself as the owner of 35 appliance stores. There and then, he committed to paying the full air time expense of the radio broadcasts on triple A time slots (the best time), and to giving all the King's Men jobs in his appliance stores to support their families while they were there. Thus it was that The King's Men collaborated to produce 500 daily radio programs which were broadcast from 5:30-6 p.m. on the Sydney station every evening as people drove home from work and listened to the radio in their cars. "So Glad I'm Yours Lord" became the signature sound.

The King's Men toured the country, spreading awareness via radio and television appearances for two years until sufficient funds were raised to purchase a property on the banks of the Nepean River in Cobbitty, NSW. With the land purchased and a band of willing volunteers

Stephen, Adelle, Craig and Glen

assembled, the work began. On the 1st of April 1961, Teen Ranch Australia was fully functioning and has been in continuous operation ever since. With the ranch established, Dr. Oswald Smith journeyed to Australia to dedicate the property. Glen and the group (with six more babies between them) returned to Canada in 1961. Tucking their ranch experience in their back pockets, they continued to travel in music ministry, returning to Australia in 1973 for the 12th anniversary.

At the time of their return to Canada in 1961, David and Norma-Jean were pioneering a church in Deep River, north of Pembroke in the Ottawa Valley. Seeing television aerials popping up on people's homes, David was inspired to investigate broadcasting possibilities with the Pembroke TV station, a CBC affiliate. He knew if he wanted to spread the love of Jesus to people who weren't in pews on

Sunday mornings, he had to find a way to reach them in their homes. When the King's Men returned to Canada, he took their LP recording into the radio station. When the TV program director heard the group on the radio, he told David how much he loved their sound. David suggested they could do a mini TV concert after the CBC news on Saturday night. Skeptical of religious broadcasting, the program director agreed but said, "No preaching, Rev. Mainse." David introduced the songs and commented aside, "It's amazing how much preaching you can get into an introduction!"

Doug Gibb with The King's Men

After the concert, the program director was thrilled with the response and said, "Let me know the next time you've got music like that and I'll put you back on the air.
David said, "I married the good music. I'll be back next week."

1962 saw the beginning of a 15-minute weekly black/white TV slot between the Saturday news and the late-night movie at the Pembroke TV station.

It wasn't until he was called Tidings Church in Sudbury Norma-Jean served from the weekly television program a larger audience.

Featuring duets and trios with Norma-Jean, David and Glen, the three had been renting the recording facilities in Hamilton, Kitchener and Barrie, but when the scope of possibilities came into focus, David challenged Glen to move to Sudbury, saying, "I need you full-time" as minister of music and to develop a chorale group for TV.

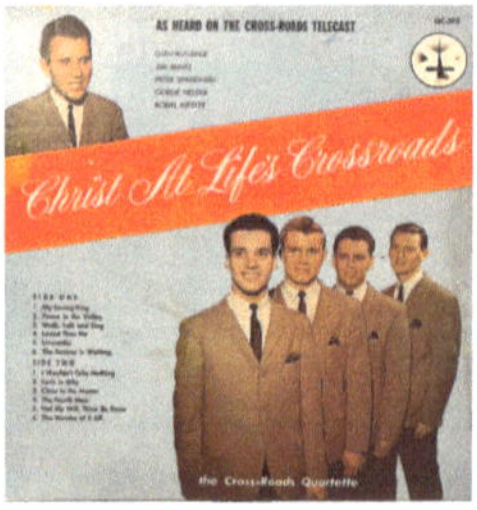

In Sudbury, they met Al Roblin, Diane's father and pastor of the Sudbury First Baptist Church. With ministerial connections, the acquaintance developed. Always slightly before his time with use of multi-media and music in the church, Al had been in broadcasting since the early days of his ministry

Rev. Al Roblin

(1939-40) at CKPR in Fort William (now Thunder Bay). During his ministry in Sudbury, he was active on both radio and on CKSO TV, a CBC affiliate. He produced *The Singing Church* 9-9:30 Sunday mornings (in which he occasionally featured Diane telling stories to a ring of children), *Hum-Along* 10-11 p.m. Sunday nights, five minutes of *Church News* twice weekly on radio, as well as 15-minute daily TV programs called *News, Views and Interviews,* five days weekly. Like David and Glen, he understood the importance of technology in reaching souls for Christ. It was in this environment of broadcast evangelism that Diane and her sister, Dona, were raised.

Diane & Zsa-Zsa

In 1963, Diane was staying overnight with a girlfriend whose father, that night, took his life by hanging, the first time suicide and its ripple effect had ever touched Diane's life. Imprinted on her mind is the memory of having to go down to the furnace room – alone – to confirm her friend's father was gone.

Although David's church had no budget to hire him, Glen agreed to move to Sudbury in 1964. He and Adelle and their three toddlers (Nadine had not yet been born) moved into the unfinished basement of David and Norma-Jean's small, three-bedroom bungalow. With the Mainse four, that made seven children in the little house, several of whom were still in diapers.

Elaine, Ronald, Reynold
and Ellen Mainse

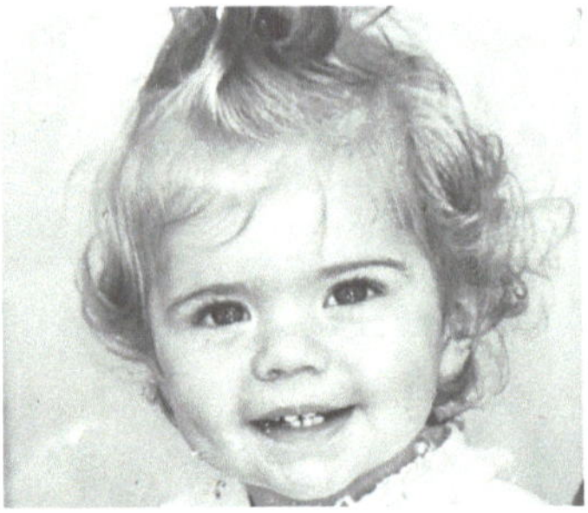

Andrea Rutledge

Glen was not on the church payroll but volunteered his time, literally digging ditches to support his young family. Living in God's economy of faith, trust and giving, it was never about the money or the applause; it was always about obedience to God's calling for ministry. Once settled, they started to record and broadcast on the Sudbury station CKSO.

It wasn't long before a small bungalow became available for rent. Glen and Adelle moved their little family out of David and Norma-Jean's basement into their own space. Wanting to help,

Glen's dad, Godfrey, sent a truckload of eight upright grand pianos from Rutledge Music to Sudbury for Glen to sell. Despite

Godfrey Rutledge

being reassured that they had reinforced the living room floor prior to unloading the pianos, the landlord was unimpressed and gave them their notice. The little bungalow became a memory in the Rutledge scrapbook.

When Al Roblin moved to Toronto in 1965, Glen took over his Sunday night radio program, "Hum-Along," another thread in the LifeNet history.

Realizing the TV program he had begun in Pembroke would go coast to coast, David told Glen, "We've got to have a name." Glen said, "It's 'Crossroads.'" He had tucked the name in the back of his mind when singing at a restaurant of the same name in Detroit, Michigan. David agreed. At this time, although Crossroads still existed as a public-service program, it went coast-to-coast across Canada with no cost for air-time.

In 1968, Glen moved to London Gospel Temple as minister of music and youth, and David accepted the call to minister at Bethel Pentecostal Church in Hamilton. Glen had been in London for two years when David asked him to go to Hamilton so they could work together more closely. This recognition of the joint call to ministry was temporarily delayed while David went out on the road in evangelism and, in 1971, Glen moved to Edmonton as minister of music.

David and Glen

Also in 1968, Al Roblin accepted the call to minister in Hamilton at Mount Calvary Baptist Church. That year, Diane married. No one could have imagined the grief that would ensue from that 38-year marriage, nor how it would serve as the foundation for her eventual calling to help build LifeNet Ministries.

While in Edmonton in 1973, Glen assisted at the funeral of Timmy, a 12-yr-old boy from a broken home who took his own life. He was, at that time, the youngest recorded suicide in Edmonton. Shattered by the tragedy of the situation, the experience changed the trajectory of Glen's life. He called David and passionately communicated the need to get to all the struggling, confused Timmys. David agreed and said, "Get home. I can't do it alone." It was Glen's depth of compassion for confused, troubled young people and his desire to introduce them to the love of Jesus that served as the catalyst for Crossroads' entrance into children's TV and ranch ministry.

Andrea, Glen, Adelle, Nadine, Craig and Stephen

Little did anyone know, at the time, that Diane's precious little Timmy was being abused by a trusted individual. As he grew a little older, he wrote heartbreaking notes about how he wanted to die. The abuse continued until he was 12-years-old and brave enough to tell Diane and her husband. As a loving mom who had stayed home to raise her children, Diane was broken by the evil ability of a predator to violate her son and manipulate her family. Years later, when she was steeped in research about abuse, determined to raise awareness and not allow her family to have suffered in vain, it became clear that the majority of people who take their lives have experienced abuse. It was more hard, preparative knowledge for the building of LifeNet.

Still in 1973, David went to the Crossroads Board of Directors and got the approval to go to the Partners of the ministry to share the great need for a children's television program. The Partners embraced the vision. A young man from London Gospel Tabernacle named the program "Circle Square."

Glen returned to Ontario where David made him producer of Crossroads and executive producer of Circle Square so he could begin working on the children's program.

Besides the production responsibilities, Glen was on-air and traveling, singing. Everybody wore a lot of hats in those early days. One of Glen's jobs involved PR, going to the affiliated TV stations to make sure they were happy with the contents of the programs and finding more stations that would carry it.

One day he was at CFTO TV in Toronto, talking to program director Jack Ruttle. Jack said to tell David that the station was going full-colour and he wanted a half-hour from Crossroads. As they discussed development, Glen gave Jack his idea for doing a montage of current world events for the opener. One of the creative team members suggested that cut #3 from an album called "Butterfly" would work. It was a drum solo and became the bed for the full-colour video montage opener for the new half-hour Crossroads program.

It was the turning point. Jack said, "If you can produce a weekly half-hour program in full-colour, you can have the 9 a.m. Sunday time-slot on Channel 9 (a CTV affiliate) until hell freezes over." That promise was good until the American religious organizations set their sights northward and arrived with bags of cash to buy time. It was at that point that hell froze over and Crossroads lost its public service status.

In 1974, the Circle Square program started and continued until 1989 on Saturdays and Sundays. In the beginning, Glen Rutledge and Ruby Peckford were the hosts of the telecast, but in 1975, Glen developed the character "Dirk," a beloved school caretaker to be played by brother Reynold Rutledge. Ann Hilsden did a fabulous job as music director. In the first six months, over 7000 children responded, requesting the free song book and sharing the needs of their hearts.

Dirk (Reynold Rutledge) and the Circle Square gang.

On Saturday mornings, Diane's Timmy and his little brother Todd (who now serves on the Advisory Council of LifeNet) would sit on the floor in front of the TV and sing along with the Circle Square kids, "Come together, come together and let your light shine."

Filming happened in the studios in Ottawa until the Confederation Life building was acquired in a 19 year/10 months lease agreement at *100 Huntley Street* in Toronto in 1977. The Global Network transmitted from the CN Tower and because the telecasts were sent through a

Confederation Life building, 100 Huntley Street, Toronto

The 100 Huntley Street Trio

cable under the streets of Toronto, the closer they were to the CN Tower, the less expensive it was. Studios were built and state-of-the-art equipment was acquired.

In 1977, 15 years after the first 15-minute *Crossroads* TV program was broadcast, *Crossroads* went from a half-hour weekly program to 90-minutes daily with the launching of "*100 Huntley Street*," Canada's first Christian daily TV broadcast on Global Television.

All the years of faithful, small steps and personal sacrifice began to bear amazing fruit. David's vision was expanded to a global picture. He dreamt of duplicating Christian broadcasting around the world by giving free training and education to potential producers who would come to Canada and then use the cutting edge Crossroads technology in their own countries. Thus it was that the "Jeffrey Conway School of Broadcasting" graduates took their training to 82 countries of the world. In His expression of His love to the world, God unfolded tremendous missions opportunities. A detailed list of past missions projects worldwide can be found at *crossroads.ca*. God has done "... *immeasurably more than we can ask or even think according to the power that works in us.*" (Ephesians 3:20)

Nite Lite Live

"Inside Track" Teen Program

On March 17, 1977, Crossroads Christian Communications was incorporated by letters patent and became CCCI. It was the umbrella organization, not only for *100 Huntley Street*, but for *Circle Square*, *Inside Track* (the show for teens), Mainroads Publishing, *Nite Lite Live* (open-line middle-of-the-night talk show) and others.

Norma-Jean became the producer of *100 Huntley Street*, providing informative, inspirational, cutting-edge programming. In the beginning, *100 Huntley Street* was broadcast live, 90 minutes daily, for five days a week. It featured a mix of upbeat

Norma-Jean

gospel music, visiting celebrities, ordinary people with extraordinary testimonies, Bible teachers and interviews with Christian leaders. A group of ministers from a wide range of denominations comprised the core of on-air personalities and guaranteed evidence of trans-denominationalism. The program encouraged viewers to phone in for prayer requests and support. Moving traditional faith-based programming from starchy religion to freedom in a relationship with Jesus within the comfort of one's own home, the full impact on countless lives in the viewership will be known in full only at the end of this age. The program was broadcast from the television studios at *100 Huntley Street*.

From those interwoven circumstances, a television ministry that has spanned decades, was born. A fixture on the dial for Canadians - whether seeking gospel programming or simply flipping channels - it has been an oasis in the desert of the secular humanism that has increasingly pervaded our culture.

Circle Square TV

In 1978, because of the overwhelming responses to the Circle Square program in the first six months of its programming, there was an obvious need for follow-up for the kids. Having experienced the effect of the ranch in Australia, Glen had a vision for dude ranches across Canada.

Glen and David met at Square One in Toronto with Mel Stevens (originally one of The King's Men, who had started a Teen Ranch in Orangeville upon his return from Australia). They began to pray towards God's provision for dude ranches across Canada.

David interviewed Glen and Reynold Rutledge on the half-hour *Crossroads* program and laid out the vision. David spoke directly to the viewers, saying, "If you have property you'd like to donate for the development of a ranch in your province, please let us know."

Reyn and Glen and David were out west doing a telethon in Regina when a letter came in from Phil Doan, an all-Canadian rodeo champion. It was concerning a section of land he wanted to donate for a ranch in Halkirk, east of Red Deer, Alberta. Glen flew to Calgary and rented a car to check it out. In 1978, The first ranch opened and Gary Lefevre became the first ranch director in Halkirk..

Mr. Kelsey donated land at Big Clear Lake in Arden near Ottawa. When David and Glen went to visit and thank him, he sat in his big chair with tears running down his ruddy cheeks, confirming his heart's desire to give his hundred acres to help win children to Jesus.

The Severn Bridge property was next. It was not a full donation but was acquired at a good price. Bill St. Pierre and Mark Wigston were early Directors.

Reynold Rutledge

Norm Bonk served at the Wolf Creek Ranch in Saskatchewan. Nine dude ranches were established across Canada.

Reynold Rutledge served as the National Director of Circle Square Ranches for over 20 years.

The Wisdom of Grace,
by Diane Roblin-Lee
Foreword by David Mainse

In January of 1978, Diane's mother, Grace Roblin,[5] and her sister, Jessie Hogan, began to pray and fast every Monday for Diane. They could see her marriage was very difficult and it was critical for her to return to the Lord. In April, God miraculously began to stir her heart and infuse her with a hunger to know Him and to understand the purpose of life. She found *100 Huntley Street* on the TV one morning and was amazed by the testimonies. Having had no prior knowledge of the baptism in the Holy Spirit, she watched every program possible, to learn and grow. With her life fully recommitted to Jesus, she felt driven to share the joy that had replaced her lostness.

Diane Roblin-Lee

In 1979, Diane made an appointment with David Mainse to request a foreword for her book, *My Father's Child,* a combination autobiography and research book on ministers and their children. The book sought to answer the question concerning why

5. https://www.amazon.ca/Wisdom-Grace-Diane-Elaine-Roblin-Lee/dp/1896213456

some ministers were able to raise their children without rebellion, while others experienced varying degrees of challenges. The deeper message concerned the struggle to find authentic identity in Christ (hence the absence of features on the doll), the universal need in the heart of every human – made ever more poignant in the identity struggles of today's youth.

When David read the manuscript, he not only agreed to providing the foreword, but wanted to publish it through his recently opened Mainroads Publishing, the publishing division of *Crossroads*.

Diane became a frequent guest and occasional co-host with David on *100 Huntley Street.* There she met Glen, who suggested her sons would love Circle Square Ranch. With the Severn Bridge Ranch just a half-hour from their home in Argyle, Timmy and Todd spent every summer of their teen

David interviewing Grace and Al Roblin with Diane

years at the ranch. Tim's depression dissipated through prayer and the Godly atmosphere at the ranch. He became a strong, joyful young believer, playing football and boldly leading his high school Inter School Christian Fellowship group.

Between 1978 when the ranches started and 2011 when decisions were made by new leadership, 250,000 kids enjoyed the amazing life experiences at the various locations across Canada. Many lives were transformed and hundreds of the ranchers entered ministry in their adult years.

In 1982, while staying high up in the Harbour Castle Hotel in Toronto, Diane, alone in the room, looked out over the buildings sprawled below. She asked God to show her His heart for the city, and became aware of lights, all the lights lighting all the rooms in all the skyscrapers, all around and all below her. Lights, rooms and people in the rooms...Behind the lighted windows were janitors working, executives struggling, prostitutes coming in after their ordeals and young moms feeding their babies. Most were never likely to darken a church door. Experiencing the heart of God, Diane's heart began to break over the city, weeping inconsolably

at the broken desperation laid out before her. Not long after, that experience, she was invited to be a guest on *Nite Lite,* Crossroads' 2- 4:30 a.m. call-in talk show. That began seven years of hosting Nite Lite every Wednesday night. Driving down the Don Valley on her way from Argyle to Huntley St., she was always aware of the lights behind the windows of the skyscrapers along the way, and she'd say, "I'm coming" as she carried the love of Jesus where pulpits could never go. On her way out of the building at five a.m. to drive the two hours home, she would often encounter David just arriving, bleary-eyed, to begin 90 minutes on his knees before the morning program. God had shown him that there was no point going on the air if he didn't spend as much time in prayer before the broadcast as he did on-air.

In 1988, Diane was invited to join the local PTA and was shocked to discover the confusing, Godless philosophy of secular humanism being imposed on elementary students. Crawling up on her bathroom vanity, with her arms wrapped around her knees, she cried out to God. From the depths of her crushed heart, she heard, "Surely you have been brought into the Kingdom for such a time as this." Diane helped organize Edu-Action Ontario and was soon after invited to run for a provincial seat in parliament. She immersed herself in research and had tremendous opportunities for debate. The disintegration of Godly values previewed the

Candidates grilled in lively debate

coming societal chaos that would elevate suicide as the second leading cause of death among teenagers.

Around that time, the Lord wakened Glen at 5:30 in the morning and impressed Isaiah 45:2,3 on his mind: *"'I will go before you and make the crooked places straight; I will break in pieces the gates of bronze and cut the bars of iron. I will give you the treasures of darkness and hidden riches of secret places, that you may know that I, the Lord, Who call you by your name, Am the God of Israel."*

Glen then had a vision of a time when technology would wrap itself around the world and he would be able to reach the same number of kids they had reached in all the years of Circle Square, 250,000, in one day. He saw the harvest of souls as a huge field of wheat, stretching as far as the eye could see, and a red barn that had been prepared to hold the harvest. He then saw a vast company of young people, all dressed in white, as though taking up six lanes of highway, coming towards him. They approached over a hill, filling the highway, all rejoicing in the Lord and singing praises to God.

As the chaos and confusion of the cultural revolution deepened and suicide became increasingly common as an 'out' for depressed teens, the need for action came into greater focus. With the vision God had given him of a great youth harvest, Glen took some early steps, producing some powerful TV commercials (miraculously without cost), to try to address the needs. The program gained traction for awhile, but life circumstances combined to see it go by the wayside.

In 1992, Seville, Spain was home to Expo '92 and the technology that Glen had envisioned wrapping itself around the world was accelerated. David's agreement with Moody's declaration that Expo was the "greatest missions opportunity...," led Crossroads to participate in four World Expos, those being in Vancouver, Brisbane, Seville and Hanover, Germany. "The Scroll," a musical masterpiece composed by David and Norma-Jean's son-in-law, Bruce Stacey, and narrated by Malcolm Muggeridge, was the centrepiece of the Crossroads sponsored pavilions. Inside the Pavilion of Promise in Spain were three high tech theaters. Diane's Praise Productions company was engaged to go to Spain and produce "Theatre Three," where close to 1,000,000 visitors from around the world

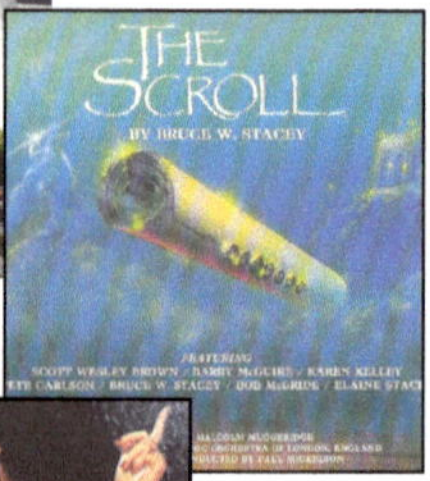

Bruce & Elaine Stacey

experienced the unfolding of the Gospel. What Great Hand of Design orchestrated Diane's humble involvement in this arena of cutting edge technology that would one day be used to reach out with hope through LifeNet?

In 1992, Crossroads moved from the rented Confederation Life building at 100 Huntley Street in Toronto, to 1295 North Service Road in the heart of Burlington, enhancing visibility and accessibility. Designed with a cozy, small-town flavour as a beacon of faith, it houses state of the art studios and equipment to broadcast hope and inspiration to the world. Now the home of the annual LifeNet banquet, it is also home to "AnyOne Pray," the Crossroads international prayer centre contracted by LifeNet to respond to LifeNet callers 24/7 across Canada and the United States.

Crossroads Unity Commons

In 1998, in a thrilling development, CTS (Crossroads Television System also founded by David) was granted a license for a 24-hour-a-day commercial television station. (CTS was re-branded as "YES TV" on Sept. 1, 2014.)

In 2006, Diane's 38-year marriage ended with devastation rooted in her husband's long-standing, hidden addiction to pornography. Staggering through her grief and loss of her home and family, Diane went back to school and became qualified as a graphic designer, a skill that would (unknowingly at the time) enable her to produce all the promotional materials for the ministry that would be "LifeNet." Grief is never a pleasant teacher, but in this case, it was necessary to deepen Diane's understanding about children and families stumbling over broken roads.

In 2007, God gave Diane a dream about a little publishing company she was to form. It was to be called, "byDesign Media."[6] Reflecting on how her whole life had been 'by design,' she registered the company exactly one year to the day of her family tragedy and hung a little sign up in her home office. Her mission statement was, "Meeting Needs by Design." Through byDesign Media, she researched and produced a nine-booklet series, *Predator-Proof Your Family* to help young parents and grandparents identify the threats of predators in their midst. The Predator series is now used as resource material for Plan to Protect[7] in over 7,500 organizations and for LifeNet Ambassadors.

Diane's 9-booklet series, Predator-Proof Your Family"

6. *www.bydesignmedia.ca*
7. Plan to Protect® provides the HIGHEST STANDARD of abuse prevention and protection to organizations servicing the vulnerable sector. www.plantoprotect.com

In 2011, *Crossroads*, planned to publish a book by Dr. Jerry Johnston and asked Diane to edit it. The book was called, *Why They Die: Curing the Death Wish in our Kids.*[8] *Crossroads* subsequently produced a two-week emphasis on addressing the pandemic of suicide amongst teens.[9] David Mainse commented, "This book motivates me to loving action on behalf of our teens. Every parent or grandparent needs to understand what is going on in the minds of today's youth."[10] It took him back to 1973 when Glen assisted at the Edmonton funeral of Timmy, the 12-yr-old boy who took his own life. It was the tragedy of that event that illuminated the need for development of the *Crossroads'* children's programming.

Dr. Gerry Tonn

In 2015 at Cedarview Church in Paris, Pastor Gerry Tonn approached Glen and David and began a conversation about Glen's brokenness for young people having been the catalyst for Crossroads starting the Circle Square TV and ranches across Canada. That conversation stirred the vision for LifeNet once more. Shortly after that meeting, David (living next door to Glen at Braeside) called Glen over to his cottage. He said, "What you did 30 years ago, you need to do again." David was referencing the early steps Glen had taken to fulfill the vision

8. https://www.amazon.ca/Why-They-Die-Curing-Death/dp/1896930506

9. Link https://youtu.be/V1QiJnqx6G8?si=oa7ueYIJWuAjaPFS

10. Mainse, David, *This Far by Faith*, CCCI, 2013, Burlington ON, p.26

God had given him for a great youth harvest. Glen replied, "Not in a million years. I'm older than Moses." He added, "By the way, do you know Bill Fletcher? He just moved in next door to me." David said, "I have 100 percent confidence in Bill Fletcher. Go tell him I have 100 percent confidence in him."

Bill Fletcher

So Glen did just that, little knowing that Bill had been in God's plan all along. It wasn't long before he joined the LifeNet Board and was invited to become the Chair. Bill's wisdom, brotherly hugs, and experience as co-founder with his wife Rachelle of *The Goodness Project* which delivers help and hope across Canada, the US and Israel, have been invaluable to LifeNet. Rachelle eventually narrated the LifeNet promotional video.

RachelleFletcher

Despite his age (born in 1936), the calling had never lost its grip on Glen's heart and mind. His memory of seeing little Timmy in his coffin in Edmonton had never faded. This time calling it "LifeNet" (a name given to him by a young man to whom God had spoken), Glen began to pull the strings together again.

David agreed to be on the first Board with Bill Fletcher (Chair), Paul Firminger and Jonathan Running.

July 13, 2016, Glen obtained incorporation and CRA charitable status for LifeNet Ministries. The Letters of Incorporation were signed by Board members David Mainse, Bill Fletcher, Paul Firminger and Glen.

Confirming the way ahead, God once again impressed a scripture on Glen's mind. This time it was Job 29:15-17. He again provided supernatural evidence of His presence by having Glen's first wife, Adelle, open her Bible to the passage just prior to Glen requesting that she read aloud what was on her page, knowing it would be the scripture God had given him. Sure enough, Adelle read...

"I was eyes to the blind, and I was feet to the lame.
I was a father to the poor, and I searched out the case
that I did not know. I broke the fangs of the wicked,
and plucked the victim from his teeth."

Adelle Rutledge

The ensuing couple of years were extraordinarily difficult with the passing of David in 2017 and the passing of Adelle in 2019. They were years of intense care-giving and focus on family.

By 2020, David's reminder of God's calling was resonating increasingly in Glen's thoughts, and the vision he had been given

for reaching vulnerable youth was, again, returning into sharp focus. God had told him that the time was now, with suicide being the second leading cause of death for teens. God had shown him how technology would wrap itself around the world, making people more connected but more isolated than they had ever been in the history of the world. Social media was destroying teens - but God had a plan for using it to reach them.

Needing help with the articulation of the vision statement, in November 2020, Glen called Diane, by now an author/co-author of over 30 books.[11] With her deep roots in *Crossroads*, she obviously shared the heart of the ministry.

While Glen had had some knowledge of Diane's journey in the intervening years between her work at *Crossroads* and her present situation, he had no depth of understanding of how God had uniquely prepared her for the work of building LifeNet. Beyond her writing and graphic skills, she had become qualified as a video producer and publisher. The personal

---

11. *www.bydesignmedia.ca*

circumstances through which God had led her had given her a heart for troubled teens and clear understanding of the cultural revolution leading to so much societal chaos.

Once the vision statement was in shape, Glen and Diane continued to talk. Diane was wintering in Mexico and the phone lines began to heat up. Glen declared his love March 11, 2021. With no question in their minds that God meant for them to be together, they were married in Mexico, April 29, and again back in Canada June 12, 2021. At their ages, there wasn't a lot of time to waste! When it was discovered that Diane was a third cousin to Adelle, it was the cherry on top for Glen's children - a gracious little surprise from God.

April 29, 2021 - Progreso, Mexico

June 12, 2021, Paris, Ontario

Once back in Canada, Diane was invited to join the LifeNet Board as CEO. With suicide increasingly prevalent among teens, Glen and Diane and the Board began building LifeNet in a very intentional way, with full confidence that the battle belongs to the Lord and He is leading the way.

We've come this far by faith!

MISSION STATEMENT

LifeNet Ministries Inc. is a federally chartered, non-profit charity. With deep concern regarding the confusion and desperation of many of today's teens (as evidenced by epidemic proportion suicide statistics), LifeNet Ministries is a Christian organization reaching out to respond to the needs of today's youth and families through collaboration with like-minded ministries and re-tooling the power of media. In partnership with concerned individuals and organizations, our desire is to act as a preemptive strike against tragedy and impact the lives of our young people with a positive message of hope.

GOALS & OBJECTIVES

1) To provide a peer-to-peer platform for youth, with hope and answers for those who have given up or who are searching for purpose, belonging and direction.

2) To build social connectedness for youth; especially for emotionally or spiritually isolated youth who have limited social supports.

3) To develop resources and tools for the building of strong teens and families.

4) To leverage hope and resilience through directing young people to proven, like-minded social media platforms already in existence (such as Teen Alpha and Youth Unlimited).

5) To develop creative productions, seminars and events to reach out to troubled youth and families, while continuing to work alongside like-minded ministries.

DEVELOPMENTS SO FAR:

- We have a faithful team of prayer warriors

- We have a 24/7 call centre/prayer line covering Canada and the US via the Crossroads AnyOne Pray group 1-855-691-5350

- We've produced a comprehensive website addressing the needs of both teens and families *www.lifenet4hope.com*

- Our growing Ambassador Team is taking root, spreading the mandate of LifeNet within their individual spheres of life

- As of 2024, we have hosted three annual fundraising banquets of well over 100 people each

- We've initiated a wristband ministry (with imprinted website url)

- We've begun international expansion with an active Board in Mexico and ambassadors in England, Texas, Costa Rica and numerous Canadian provinces

- Implementation of two yearly initiatives
  * Move-a-thon fundraiser
  * World Day of Prayer for Youth Suicide Prevention

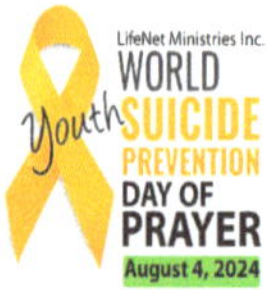

- Development of a Facebook Page

- Development of an Ambassador Page

- Development of a team of Social Media Warriors to spread hope and wage a preemptive strike against tragedy

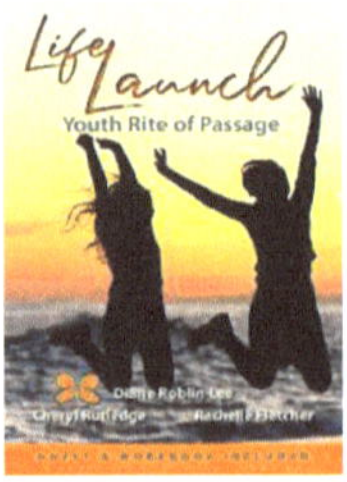

- Development of the *LifeLaunch* Rite-of-Passage to help transition young teens successfully into adulthood with a book/ workbook available on Amazon and updated for use in youth groups

- Development of *The Family LifeNet*, a book/ workbook with tips, strategies and tools for strengthening today's families

Seminars with:
Dr. Gerry Tonn
Dr. David Dwarka
Dr. Francis Oduro

- Working with three Christian psychotherapists to organize and provide mental health seminars across Canada

Cheryl Ruledge

- The appointment of an Executive Coordinator for the Ambassador Team
  Cheryl Rutledge

Pam Taylor

- The appointment of a church and youth group Information Coordinator - Pam Taylor

Seneca Bates

- The engagement of admin assistant Seneca Bates

- Updated Board:

Glen Rutledge
Founder

Bill Fletcher
Chair

Diane Roblin-Rutledge
CEO

Gary Vaters
Vice-Chair

David Dwarka
Seminars

Al Linton
Sec/Treasurer

Victor Barrera
Mexico

- The development of an Advisory Council comprised of:

Dr. Gerry Tonn
Psychotherapist
& liaison with
Youth Leaders

Stevan Novoselac
Chair of
Crossroads and
YES TV

Todd W. Lee
Google
Senior
Developer

Sonya & Kenny
Sault
First Nations
Advisors

The history of the development of LifeNet, interwoven through the history of Circle Square TV, Circle Square Ranches, and Crossroads Christian Communications Inc. is a tremendous story of the faithfulness and love of God for today's teens and families.

LifeNet
MINISTRIES®

www.lifenet4hope.com

For Such a Time as This

The Interwoven History of LifeNet, Crossroads,
100 Huntley Street, Circle Square TV and Circle Square Ranches

If you were moved by the demonstration of
the hand of God in directing the building of LifeNet,
He may be nudging you to help us
reach today's young people with hope.

Here are a few suggestions for how you can help:

Watch our promo video on the "About" page of our website.

Show a teen you really care. Listen. Smile. Spend time. Pray.

Mention the ministry on social media and "like" us on Facebook.

Host a LifeLaunch celebration for a teen. (See LifeLaunch guide.)

Share our website with families and young people
www.lifenet4hope.com

Pray about joining our prayer team.

Pray about becoming a LifeNet Ambassador.
For more info and downloadable application, go to
www.lifenet4hope.com/support

Consider donating through the "Donate" button on our website.

Thanks for reading!

The LifeNet Team

byDesign MEDIA